A ROSARY LITANY

Fr. Edward Looney

Our Sunday Visitor
www.osv.com
Our Sunday Visitor Publishing Division
Our Sunday Visitor, Inc.
Huntington, Indiana 46750

Nihil Obstat
Fr. John W. Girotti

Imprimatur
✠ David L. Ricken, DD, JCL
Bishop of Green Bay
January 25, 2016

Our Sunday Visitor Publishing Division
Our Sunday Visitor, Inc.
200 Noll Plaza
Huntington, IN 46750
1-800-348-2440

ISBN: 978-1-68192-337-6 (Inventory No. T2019)

eISBN: 978-1-68192-338-3
LCCN: 2018950686

Cover and interior design: Lindsey Riesen
Cover art: Shutterstock

Interior art: Caroline Baker-Mazure

PRINTED IN THE UNITED STATES OF AMERICA

The Rationale Behind
A Rosary Litany

The Rosary, popularized by the sons of Saint Dominic, has been a devotion of the Christian faithful for centuries. Unfortunately, in the third millennium, many people have become dissatisfied with the Rosary as a form of meditation and prayer, viewing it as old-fashioned and outdated.

The Rosary itself is scriptural by nature, containing the Our Father and the angelic salutation (Hail Mary), in addition to the mysteries rooted in sacred Scripture. Moreover, the Rosary has been called a compendium to the Gospels as it leads us through the life of Jesus and Mary. In it, Mary leads us to reflect on the life of the Savior, from his birth through his public ministry, to his passion, death, and resurrection.

The rhythm of the Rosary is not repetitive as some may contend; rather, the repetition lends itself to meditation. As we pray each of the decades, we get lost in the reflection of the mystery. Thus the repetition of the Hail Mary allows the mystery to consume the devotee.

Perhaps in our technological era, which is consumed by noise, people are no longer able to be still for twenty minutes to bring themselves into the presence of God and reflect. It has become difficult to meditate on one thing for a short amount of time because our thoughts are fleeting and the worries of life distract us. That is why, in recent years, Rosary devotional books have been written — to assist in the meditative and contemplative aspect of the Rosary.

This small devotional book, *A Rosary Litany*, reintroduces the Christian faithful to an old custom of praying the Rosary. Saint Louis-Marie Grignion de Montfort, in *The Secret of the Rosary*, proposed for devotional purposes the addition of a meditative element to the Hail Mary prayer.

Popes Paul VI, in *Marialis Cultus*, and John Paul II, in *Rosarium Virginis Mariae*, also encouraged this devotion. These additional phrases guide and focus the meditation of the mystery within the context of the Hail Mary.

In each decade of *A Rosary Litany*, the de Montfort suggestion is provided, in addition to several other invocations that could be inserted after the name of Jesus or Mary. When prayed in succession, the Rosary becomes like a litany, on account of the varied invocations.

How to Use
A Rosary Litany

Saint Louis de Montfort encouraged the addition of one phrase, which is listed separately from the ten other phrases proposed by this book for directed meditation. If one would like to use the Saint Louis de Montfort suggestion, simply omit one of the ten listed. Also, it should be noted that the Luminous Mysteries were added by Pope St. John Paul II in 2002, so there is no suggested phrase from Saint Louis de Montfort. Some mysteries contain alternative invocations which could be substituted for those enumerated.

Some invocations are written in the style using the word "who." These invocations could be rephrased at the discretion of the devotee. "Thy womb Jesus, who met John the Baptist" could be modified to "thy womb Jesus, meeting John the Baptist"; or "thy womb Jesus, who prayed all might be one" could be modified to "thy womb Jesus, praying all might be one."

Here are three different ways *A Rosary Litany* could be used:

1. All ten invocations for each mystery could be used during the recitation of the Rosary. In this way, the devotion truly becomes like a litany. When praying each of the ten Hail Marys, insert the "litany invocation" after "thy womb Jesus" or "Mother of God." In some cases, the Marian reference modifies "Holy Mary, Mother of God."

2. A person could choose to use one or two of the phrases at one time, thereby spreading the phrases over a period of a few weeks. The repetition of a specific phrase over and over again makes it resonate within the prayerful meditation. In one sense, the invocation becomes an earnest plea or desire. It is possible that while you use *A Rosary Litany* a certain invocation may become your favorite and you will use it every time when reflecting on the mystery.

3. Saint John Paul recommended this practice for the public recitation of the Rosary. There are two ways which this can be accomplished. First, the leader may invoke the name

of Jesus and the additional clause, and everyone else picks up with "Holy Mary, Mother of God." When the clause comes after Mary's name, the group could lead the first part of the Hail Mary, and the leader, the second part with the modifying phrase. If each person praying the Rosary has a book to guide them, a second way is possible; the entire group can begin with the clause after Jesus' name, continuing then with the rest of the Hail Mary.

Let us pray that this small Rosary devotional can help renew devotion to Our Lady's Rosary, for it is a tried-and-true devotion of our faith.

As a Gospel prayer, centered on the mystery of the redemptive Incarnation, the Rosary is therefore a prayer with a clearly Christological orientation. Its most characteristic element, in fact, the litany-like succession of Hail Marys, becomes in itself an unceasing praise of Christ, who is the ultimate object both of the angel's announcement and of the greeting of the mother of John the Baptist: "Blessed is the fruit of your womb" (Lk 1:42). We would go further and say that the succession of Hail Marys constitutes the wrap on which is woven the contemplation of the mysteries. The Jesus that each Hail Mary recalls is the same Jesus whom the succession of the mysteries proposes to us — now as the Son of God, now as the Son of the Virgin — at his birth in a stable at Bethlehem, at his presentation by his mother in the Temple, as a youth full of zeal for his Father's affairs, as the Redeemer in agony in the garden, scourged and crowned with thorns, carrying the cross and dying on Calvary, risen from the dead and ascended to the glory of the Father to send forth the gift of the Spirit. *As is well known, at one time there was a custom, still preserved in certain places, of adding to the name of Jesus in each Hail Mary reference to the mystery being contemplated. And this was done precisely in order to help contemplation and to make the mind and the voice act in unison.*

— Paul VI, *Marialis Cultus,*
46 (emphasis added)

The center of gravity in the Hail Mary, the hinge as it were which joins its two parts, is the name of Jesus. Sometimes, in hurried recitation, this center of gravity can be overlooked, and with it the connection to the mystery of Christ being contemplated. Yet it is precisely the emphasis given to the name of Jesus and to his mystery that is the sign of a meaningful and fruitful recitation of the Rosary. Pope Paul VI drew attention, in his apostolic exhortation *Marialis Cultus,* to the custom in certain regions of highlighting the name of Christ by the addition of a clause referring to the mystery being contemplated. *This is a praiseworthy custom, especially during public recitation. It gives forceful expression to our faith in Christ, directed to the different moments of the Redeemer's life. It is at once a profession of faith and an aid in concentrating our meditation, since it facilitates the process of assimilation to the mystery of Christ inherent in the repetition of the Hail Mary.* When we repeat the name of Jesus — the only name given to us by which we may hope for salvation (cf. Acts 4:12) — in close association with the name of his Blessed Mother, almost as if it were done at her suggestion, we set out on a path of assimilation meant to help us enter more deeply into the life of Christ.

— John Paul II, *Rosarium Virginis Mariae*, 33 (emphasis added)

JOYFUL MYSTERIES

*Traditionally prayed on
Mondays and Saturdays*

1. Annunciation

De Montfort suggestion: Jesus incarnate

1. thy womb, Jesus, **announced by the angel Gabriel**. Holy Mary, Mother of God, pray for us sinners …

2. thy womb, Jesus, **conceived by the Holy Spirit**. Holy Mary, Mother of God, pray for us sinners …

3. thy womb, Jesus, **Son of the Most High**. Holy Mary, Mother of God, pray for us sinners …

4. thy womb, Jesus, **ruler of the House of Jacob**. Holy Mary, Mother of God, pray for us sinners …

5. thy womb, Jesus, **whose kingdom will have no end**. Holy Mary, Mother of God, pray for us sinners …

6. thy womb, Jesus. Holy Mary, Mother of God, **spouse of the Holy Spirit,** pray for us sinners …

7. thy womb, Jesus. Holy Mary, Mother of God, **chosen by God**, pray for us sinners …

8. thy womb, Jesus. Holy Mary, Mother of God, **handmaid of the Lord,** pray for us sinners …

9. thy womb, Jesus. Holy Mary, Mother of God, **overshadowed by the Holy Spirit**, pray for us sinners …

10. thy womb, Jesus. Holy Mary, Mother of God, **Ark of the New Covenant**, pray for us sinners …

Alternative Invocations
— thy womb, Jesus, **dwelling in the womb of the Virgin**. Holy Mary, Mother of God, pray for us sinners ...

— thy womb, Jesus. Holy Mary, Mother of God, **betrothed to Joseph**, pray for us sinners ...

— thy womb, Jesus. Holy Mary, Mother of God, **who pondered the angel's greeting**, pray for us sinners ...

2. Visitation of Mary to Elizabeth

De Montfort suggestion: Jesus sanctifying

1. thy womb, Jesus. Holy Mary, Mother of God, **who went in haste to visit Elizabeth**, pray for us sinners …

2. thy womb, Jesus, **who met John the Baptist**. Holy Mary, Mother of God, pray for us sinners …

3. thy womb, Jesus, **the cause of John's joy**. Holy Mary Mother of God, pray for us sinners …

4. thy womb, Jesus, **recognized as Lord by Elizabeth**. Holy Mary, Mother of God, pray for us sinners …

5. thy womb, Jesus. Holy Mary, Mother of God, **woman of charity**, pray for us sinners …

6. thy womb, Jesus. Holy Mary, Mother of God, **proclaimed blessed by Elizabeth**, pray for us sinners …

7. thy womb, Jesus. Holy Mary, Mother of **our Lord and** God, pray for us sinners …

8. thy womb, Jesus. Holy Mary, Mother of God, **who believed what was spoken to her**, pray for us sinners …

9. thy womb, Jesus. Holy Mary, Mother of God, **who magnified the Lord**, pray for us sinners …

10. thy womb, Jesus. Holy Mary, Mother of God, **who remained with Elizabeth three months**, pray for us sinners …

3. BIRTH OF JESUS
De Montfort suggestion: Jesus born
in poverty

1. thy womb, Jesus, **born for us in Bethlehem**. Holy Mary, Mother of God, pray for us sinners …

2. thy womb, Jesus, **who is Emmanuel**. Holy Mary, Mother of God, pray for us sinners …

3. thy womb, Jesus, **Son of God and son of Mary**. Holy Mary, Mother of God, pray for us sinners …

4. thy womb, Jesus, **wrapped in swaddling clothes**. Holy Mary, Mother of God, pray for us sinners …

5. thy womb, Jesus, **laid in a manger**. Holy Mary, Mother of God, pray for us sinners …

6. thy womb, Jesus, **visited by shepherds and magi**. Holy Mary, Mother of God, pray for us sinners …

7. thy womb, Jesus, **born to save us from our sins**. Holy Mary, Mother of God, pray for us sinners …

8. thy womb, Jesus. Holy Mary, Mother of God, **who held the child Jesus**, pray for us sinners …

9. thy womb, Jesus. Holy Mary, Mother of God, **whose womb bore the Son of God**, pray for us sinners …

10. thy womb, Jesus. Holy Mary, Mother of God, **who nursed the child Jesus**, pray for us sinners …

Alternative Invocation
— thy womb, Jesus, Holy Mary, Mother of God, **ever Virgin**, pray for us sinners …

ALTERNATIVE INVOCATIONS INSPIRED BY THE GOSPEL OF JOHN CHAPTER I

— thy womb, Jesus, **Word made flesh**. Holy Mary, Mother of God, pray for us sinners …

— thy womb, Jesus, **who made his dwelling among us**. Holy Mary, Mother of God, pray for us sinners …

— thy womb, Jesus, **who was full of grace and truth**. Holy Mary, Mother of God, pray for us sinners …

— thy womb, Jesus, **from whom we have all received grace in place of grace**. Holy Mary, Mother of God, pray for us sinners …

— thy womb, Jesus, **who is the Light that shines in darkness**, Holy Mary, Mother of God, pray for us sinners …

— thy womb, Jesus, **who is the True Light, which enlightens everyone**. Holy Mary, Mother of God, pray for us sinners …

4. PRESENTATION IN THE TEMPLE

De Montfort suggestion: Jesus sacrificed

1. thy womb, Jesus, **presented in the Temple**. Holy Mary, Mother of God, pray for us sinners …

2. thy womb, Jesus, **offered to the Father**. Holy Mary, Mother of God, pray for us sinners …

3. thy womb, Jesus, **the fulfillment of Simeon's mission**. Holy Mary, Mother of God, pray for us sinners …

4. thy womb, Jesus, **the light of revelation**. Holy Mary, Mother of God, pray for us sinners …

5. thy womb, Jesus, **destined for the fall and rise of many**. Holy Mary, Mother of God, pray for us sinners ...

6. thy womb, Jesus, **a sign of contradiction**. Holy Mary, Mother of God, pray for us sinners ...

7. thy womb, Jesus, **proclaimed to others by the prophetess Anna**. Holy Mary, Mother of God, pray for us sinners ...

8. thy womb, Jesus. Holy Mary, Mother of God, **whose heart was pierced by a sword**, pray for us sinners ...

9. thy womb, Jesus. Holy Mary, Mother of God, **the contemplating Virgin**, pray for us sinners ...

10. thy womb, Jesus. Holy Mary, Mother of God, **who was purified**, pray for us sinners ...

5. FINDING OF JESUS IN THE TEMPLE

De Montfort suggestion: Jesus,
Saint among saints

1. thy womb, Jesus, **who accompanied his parents to the Temple**. Holy Mary, Mother of God, pray for us sinners …

2. thy womb, Jesus, **who remained behind in Jerusalem**. Holy Mary, Mother of God, pray for us sinners …

3. thy womb, Jesus, **who was found in the Temple**. Holy Mary, Mother of God, pray for us sinners …

4. thy womb, Jesus, **who was sitting among the teachers**. Holy Mary, Mother of God, pray for us sinners …

5. thy womb, Jesus, **who asked questions of the rabbis**. Holy Mary, Mother of God, pray for us sinners …

6. thy womb, Jesus, **who was about his Father's business**. Holy Mary, Mother of God, pray for us sinners …

7. thy womb, Jesus. Holy Mary, Mother of God, **who searched for Jesus**, pray for us sinners …

8. thy womb, Jesus. Holy Mary, Mother of God, **worried for her son**, pray for us sinners …

9. thy womb, Jesus. Holy Mary, Mother of God, **who asked, "Why have you done this to us?"** pray for us sinners …

10. thy womb, Jesus. Holy Mary, Mother of God, **who kept these things in her heart,** pray for us sinners …

ALTERNATIVE INVOCATIONS

— thy womb, Jesus, **obedient to his family in Nazareth**. Holy Mary, Mother of God, pray for us sinners …

— thy womb, Jesus. Holy Mary, Mother of God, **puzzled by Jesus' response**, pray for us sinners …

LUMINOUS MYSTERIES

Traditionally prayed on Thursdays

1. Baptism in the River Jordan

1. thy womb, Jesus, **baptized by John**. Holy Mary, Mother of God, pray for us sinners …

2. thy womb, Jesus, **who entered the River Jordan**. Holy Mary, Mother of God, pray for us sinners …

3. thy womb, Jesus, **who must increase in us**. Holy Mary, Mother of God, pray for us sinners …

4. thy womb, Jesus, **on whom a dove descended**. Holy Mary, Mother of God, pray for us sinners …

5. thy womb, Jesus, **in whom the Father is well pleased**. Holy Mary, Mother of God, pray for us sinners …

6. thy womb, Jesus, **the beloved Son**. Holy Mary, Mother of God, pray for us sinners …

7. thy womb, Jesus, **who is the one mightier than John**. Holy Mary, Mother of God, pray for us sinners …

8. thy womb, Jesus, **who will baptize with the Holy Spirit and fire**. Holy Mary, Mother of God, pray for us sinners …

9. thy womb, Jesus, **who sent his disciples to baptize.** Holy Mary, Mother of God, pray for us sinners …

10. thy womb, Jesus, **who is the Living Water**. Holy Mary, Mother of God, pray for us sinners …

ALTERNATIVE INVOCATIONS EMPHASIZING JESUS' TEMPTATION IN THE DESERT

— thy womb, Jesus, **who was led by the Spirit**. Holy Mary, Mother of God, pray for us sinners …

— thy womb, Jesus, **who fasted and prayed**. Holy Mary, Mother of God, pray for us sinners …

— thy womb, Jesus, **who triumphed over the devil and his temptations**. Holy Mary, Mother of God, pray for us sinners …

2. WEDDING FEAST AT CANA

1. thy womb, Jesus, **invited to the wedding feast**. Holy Mary, Mother of God, pray for us sinners …

2. thy womb, Jesus, **who learned of the wine shortage from Mary**. Holy Mary, Mother of God, pray for us sinners …

3. thy womb, Jesus, **whose hour had not yet come**. Holy Mary, Mother of God, pray for us sinners …

4. thy womb, Jesus, **who commanded the servants to bring six jars of water**. Holy Mary, Mother of God, pray for us sinners …

5. thy womb, Jesus, **who turned water into wine**. Holy Mary, Mother of God, pray for us sinners …

6. thy womb, Jesus, **in whom his disciples began to believe**. Holy Mary, Mother of God, pray for us sinners …

7. thy womb, Jesus, **who performed the first of his signs at Cana**. Holy Mary, Mother of God, pray for us sinners …

8. thy womb, Jesus. Holy Mary, Mother of God, **attentive to the needs of others**, pray for us sinners …

9. thy womb, Jesus. Holy Mary, Mother of God, **who interceded for the couple**, pray for us sinners …

10. thy womb, Jesus. Holy Mary, Mother of God, **who said, "Do whatever he tells you,"** pray for us sinners …

ALTERNATIVE INVOCATION
— thy womb, Jesus. Holy Mary, Mother of God, **the attentive Virgin**, pray for us sinners …

3. Proclamation of the Kingdom

1. thy womb, Jesus, **who proclaimed the Kingdom**. Holy Mary, Mother of God, pray for us sinners …

2. thy womb, Jesus, **who calls us to repentance**. Holy Mary, Mother of God, pray for us sinners …

3. thy womb, Jesus, **who taught his disciples how to pray**. Holy Mary, Mother of God, pray for us sinners …

4. thy womb, Jesus, **who taught us to forgive others**. Holy Mary, Mother of God, pray for us sinners …

5. thy womb, Jesus, **who proclaimed the Beatitude**s. Holy Mary, Mother of God, pray for us sinners …

6. thy womb, Jesus, **who came not to abolish the Law**. Holy Mary, Mother of God, pray for us sinners …

7. thy womb, Jesus, **the fulfillment of the Law**. Holy Mary, Mother of God, pray for us sinners …

8. thy womb, Jesus, **who forgives our sins**. Holy Mary, Mother of God, pray for us sinners …

9. thy womb, Jesus, **who inaugurated his ministry of mercy**. Holy Mary, Mother of God, pray for us sinners …

10. thy womb, Jesus, **who shows us the way to the Father**. Holy Mary, Mother of God, pray for us sinners …

ALTERNATIVE INVOCATION
— thy womb, Jesus, **teach us how to pray**.
Holy Mary, Mother of God, pray for us sinners …

4. Transfiguration

1. thy womb, Jesus, **who ascended Mount Tabor**. Holy Mary, Mother of God, pray for us sinners …

2. thy womb, Jesus, **accompanied by Peter, James, and John**. Holy Mary, Mother of God, pray for us sinners …

3. thy womb, Jesus, **whom it is good to be with**. Holy Mary, Mother of God, pray for us sinners …

4. thy womb, Jesus, **transfigured before his disciples**. Holy Mary, Mother of God, pray for us sinners …

5. thy womb, Jesus, **whose face was as radiant as the sun**. Holy Mary, Mother of God, pray for us sinners ...

6. thy womb, Jesus, **the beloved Son**. Holy Mary, Mother of God, pray for us sinners ...

7. thy womb, Jesus, **whom we should listen to**. Holy Mary, Mother of God, pray for us sinners ...

8. thy womb, Jesus, **who instructed the disciples to rise and not be afraid**. Holy Mary, Mother of God, pray for us sinners ...

9. thy womb, Jesus, **the Son of Man who will suffer**. Holy Mary, Mother of God, pray for us sinners ...

10. thy womb, Jesus, **the fulfillment of the Law and the prophets**. Holy Mary, Mother of God, pray for us sinners ...

ALTERNATIVE INVOCATION
— thy womb, Jesus, **appearing with Moses and Elijah**. Holy Mary, Mother of God, pray for us sinners …

5. Institution of the Holy Eucharist

1. thy womb, Jesus, **who instituted the Eucharist**. Holy Mary, Mother of God, pray for us sinners …

2. thy womb, Jesus, **present in the Eucharist**. Holy Mary, Mother of God, pray for us sinners …

3. thy womb, Jesus, **the living bread come down from heaven**. Holy Mary, Mother of God, pray for us sinners …

4. thy womb, Jesus, **true food and true drink**. Holy Mary, Mother of God, pray for us sinners …

5. thy womb, Jesus, **who took, broke, blessed, and gave the bread to his disciple**s. Holy Mary, Mother of God, pray for us sinners …

6. thy womb, Jesus, **whose blood is the New Covenant**. Holy Mary, Mother of God, pray for us sinners …

7. thy womb, Jesus, **who promises eternal life**. Holy Mary, Mother of God, pray for us sinners …

8. thy womb, Jesus, **who instructed us to do this in memory of him**· Holy Mary, Mother of God, pray for us sinners …

9. thy womb, Jesus. Holy Mary, Mother of God, **Ark of the New Covenan**t, pray for us sinners …

10. thy womb, Jesus. Holy Mary, Mother of God, **and Mother of the Eucharist**, pray for us sinners …

ALTERNATIVE INVOCATION

— thy womb, Jesus, **present body, blood, soul, and divinity.** Holy Mary, Mother of God, pray for us sinners …

SORROWFUL MYSTERIES

*Traditionally prayed on
Tuesdays and Fridays*

1. Agony in the Garden

De Montfort suggestion: Jesus in his agony

———◦◦———

1. thy womb Jesus, **agonizing in the garden**. Holy Mary, Mother of God, pray for us sinners …

2. thy womb Jesus, **praying in the garden**. Holy Mary, Mother of God, pray for us sinners …

3. thy womb Jesus, **who prayed they all may be one**. Holy Mary, Mother of God, pray for us sinners …

4. thy womb Jesus, **who prayed that this cup might pass**. Holy Mary, Mother of God, pray for us sinners …

5. thy womb, Jesus, **whose sweat became like drops of blood**. Holy Mary, Mother of God, pray for us sinners …

6. thy womb, Jesus, **who said, "Watch and pray."** Holy Mary, Mother of God, pray for us sinners …

7. thy womb, Jesus, **who found the apostles asleep**. Holy Mary, Mother of God, pray for us sinners …

8. thy womb, Jesus, **whose hour had arrived**. Holy Mary, Mother of God, pray for us sinners …

9. thy womb, Jesus, **betrayed by Judas**. Holy Mary, Mother of God, pray for us sinners …

10. thy womb, Jesus, **arrested in the garden**. Holy Mary, Mother of God, pray for us sinners …

ALTERNATIVE INVOCATIONS

— thy womb, Jesus. Holy Mary, Mother of God, **the sorrowful Mother,** pray for us sinners ...

— thy womb, Jesus, **who prayed to his Father**. Holy Mary, Mother of God, pray for us sinners ...

— thy womb, Jesus, **who prayed three times**. Holy Mary, Mother of God, pray for us sinners ... (see Mt 26:44)

2. Scourging at the Pillar

De Montfort suggestion: Jesus scourged

1. thy womb, Jesus, **scourged at the pillar**. Holy Mary, Mother of God, pray for us sinners …

2. thy womb, Jesus, **beaten and bruised**. Holy Mary, Mother of God, pray for us sinners …

3. thy womb, Jesus, **scourged for our offenses**. Holy Mary, Mother of God, pray for us sinners …

4. thy womb, Jesus, **chained to the pillar**. Holy Mary, Mother of God, pray for us sinners …

5. thy womb, Jesus, **who was in excruciating pain**. Holy Mary, Mother of God, pray for us sinners ...

6. thy womb, Jesus, **bruised by a reed**. Holy Mary, Mother of God, pray for us sinners ...

7. thy womb, Jesus, **who was spat upon**. Holy Mary, Mother of God, pray for us sinners ...

8. thy womb, Jesus, **stripped of his clothes**. Holy Mary, Mother of God, pray for us sinners ...

9. thy womb, Jesus, **clothed in purple garments**. Holy Mary, Mother of God, pray for us sinners ...

10. thy womb, Jesus. Holy Mary, Mother of God, **the sorrowful Mother,** pray for us sinners ...

3. Crowning with Thorns

De Montfort suggestion: Jesus
crowned with thorns

---

1. thy womb, Jesus, **crowned with thorns**.
Holy Mary, Mother of God, pray for us sinners ...

2. thy womb, Jesus, **King of the Jews**. Holy
Mary, Mother of God, pray for us sinners ...

3. thy womb, Jesus, **King of Kings**. Holy
Mary, Mother of God, pray for us sinners ...

4. thy womb, Jesus, **mocked by the soldiers**.
Holy Mary, Mother of God, pray for us sinners ...

5. thy womb, Jesus, **bleeding from his wounds**. Holy Mary, Mother of God, pray for us sinners …

6. thy womb, Jesus, **in excruciating pain**. Holy Mary, Mother of God, pray for us sinners …

7. thy womb, Jesus, **Lord of Lords**. Holy Mary, Mother of God, pray for us sinners …

8. thy womb, Jesus, **the Suffering Servant**. Holy Mary, Mother of God, pray for us sinners …

9. thy womb, Jesus. Holy Mary, Mother of God, **weeping for her son**, pray for us sinners …

10. thy womb, Jesus. Holy Mary, Mother of God, **the sorrowful Mother,** pray for us sinners …

ALTERNATIVE INVOCATIONS

— thy womb, Jesus, **who was handed over to Pilate**. Holy Mary, Mother of God, pray for us sinners …

— thy womb, Jesus, **who was humiliated for our offenses**. Holy Mary, Mother of God, pray for us sinners …

— thy womb, Jesus, **who was rejected by his own people**. Holy Mary, Mother of God, pray for us sinners …

— thy womb, Jesus, **behold the Man**. Holy Mary, Mother of God, pray for us sinners …

— thy womb, Jesus, **in whom Pilate could find no guilt**. Holy Mary, Mother of God, pray for us sinners …

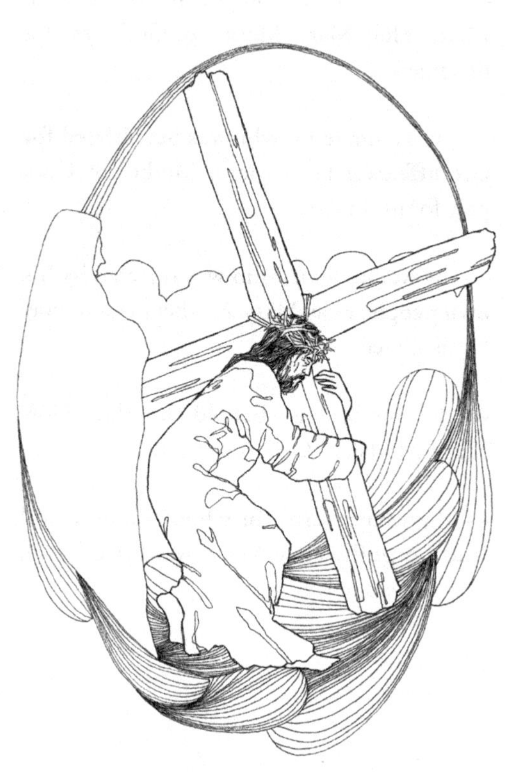

4. Carrying of the Cross

De Montfort suggestion: Jesus
carrying his cross

1. thy womb, Jesus, **who carried his cross**.
Holy Mary, Mother of God, pray for us sinners …

2. thy womb, Jesus, **who fell three times**.
Holy Mary, Mother of God, pray for us sinners …

3. thy womb, Jesus, **who met his mother**.
Holy Mary, Mother of God, pray for us sinners …

4. thy womb, Jesus, **helped by Simon of Cyrene**. Holy Mary, Mother of God, pray for us sinners …

5. thy womb, Jesus, **whose face was wiped by Veronica**. Holy Mary, Mother of God, pray for us sinners ...

6. thy womb, Jesus, **who consoled the women of Jerusalem**. Holy Mary, Mother of God, pray for us sinners ...

7. thy womb, Jesus, **stripped of his garments**. Holy Mary, Mother of God, pray for us sinners ...

8. thy womb, Jesus, **nailed to the cross**. Holy Mary, Mother of God, pray for us sinners ...

9. thy womb, Jesus, **lifted above the earth**. Holy Mary, Mother of God, pray for us sinners ...

10. thy womb, Jesus. Holy Mary, Mother of God, **the sorrowful Mother,** pray for us sinners ...

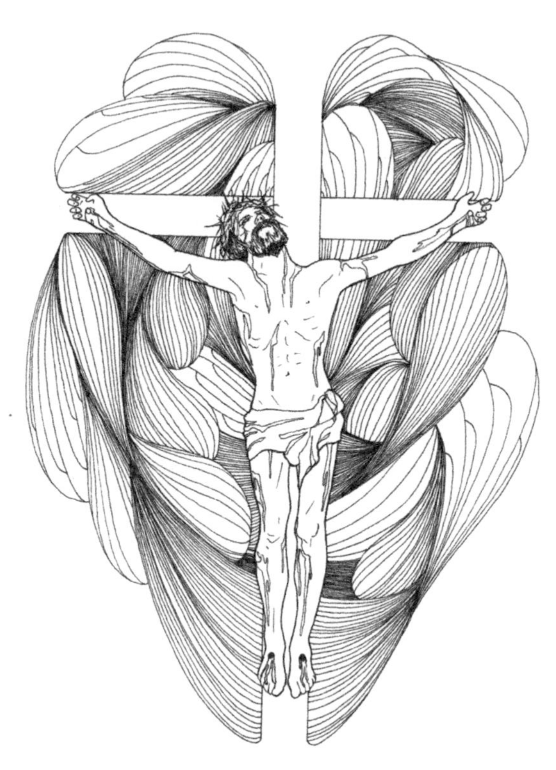

5. Crucifixion
De Montfort suggestion: Jesus crucified

---

1. thy womb, Jesus, **crucified for our offenses**. Holy Mary, Mother of God, pray for us sinners …

2. thy womb, Jesus, **who thirsts**. Holy Mary, Mother of God, pray for us sinners …

3. thy womb, Jesus, **who forgave his transgressors**. Holy Mary, Mother of God, pray for us sinners …

4. thy womb, Jesus, **who promised the Kingdom to the good thief**. Holy Mary, Mother of God, pray for us sinners …

5. thy womb, Jesus, **who entrusted Mary to John**. Holy Mary, Mother of God, pray for us sinners …

6. thy womb, Jesus, **who breathed his last**. Holy Mary, Mother of God, pray for us sinners …

7. thy womb, Jesus, **pierced in the side**. Holy Mary, Mother of God, pray for us sinners …

8. thy womb, Jesus, **from whom blood and water flowed**. Holy Mary, Mother of God, pray for us sinners …

9. thy womb, Jesus. Holy Mary, Mother of God, **standing at the foot of the cross,** pray for us sinners …

10. thy womb, Jesus. Holy Mary, Mother of God, **who held the body of Jesus,** pray for us sinners …

Alternative Invocations

— thy womb, Jesus, **hanging from the tree**. Holy Mary, Mother of God, pray for us sinners …

— thy womb, Jesus. Holy Mary, Mother of God, **the sorrowful Mother,** pray for us sinners …

— thy womb, Jesus. Holy Mary, **the desolate Mother of God**, pray for us sinners …

GLORIOUS MYSTERIES

*Traditionally prayed on Sundays
and Wednesdays*

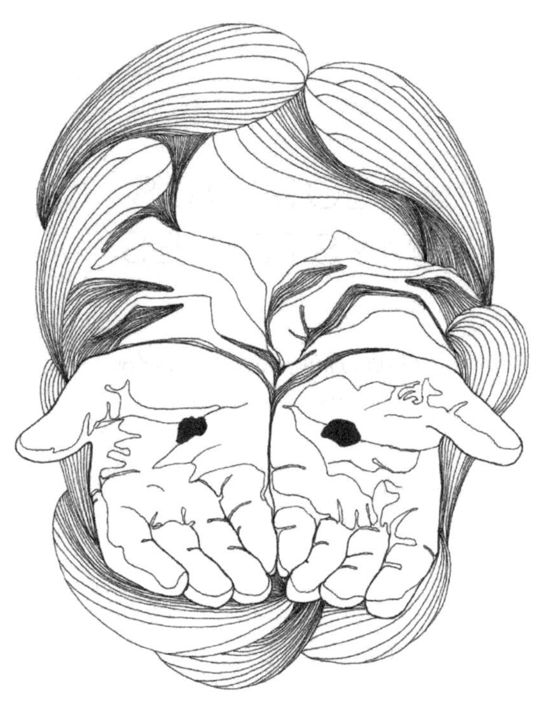

1. Resurrection
De Montfort suggestion: Jesus risen
from the dead

---

1. thy womb, Jesus, **risen from the dead**. Holy Mary, Mother of God, pray for us sinners …

2. thy womb, Jesus, **whose tomb was empty**. Holy Mary, Mother of God, pray for us sinners …

3. thy womb, Jesus, **who defeated death**. Holy Mary, Mother of God, pray for us sinners …

4. thy womb, Jesus, **who appeared to Mary Magdalene**. Holy Mary, Mother of God, pray for us sinners …

5. thy womb, Jesus, **who revealed himself on the road to Emmaus**. Holy Mary, Mother of God, pray for us sinners …

6. thy womb, Jesus, **who entered through the locked door**. Holy Mary, Mother of God, pray for us sinners …

7. thy womb, Jesus, **whom Thomas doubted**. Holy Mary, Mother of God, pray for us sinners …

8. thy womb, Jesus, **who fed his disciples**. Holy Mary, Mother of God, pray for us sinners …

9. thy womb, Jesus, **who asked Peter, "Do you love me?"** Holy Mary, Mother of God, pray for us sinners …

10. thy womb, Jesus. Holy Mary, Mother of God, **the rejoicing Mother,** pray for us sinners …

ALTERNATIVE INVOCATION

— thy womb, Jesus, **whose garments were found in the tomb**. Holy Mary, Mother of God, pray for us sinners …

2. ASCENSION
De Montfort suggestion: Jesus
ascending to heaven

---

1. thy womb, Jesus, **who ascended into heaven**. Holy Mary, Mother of God, pray for us sinners …

2. thy womb, Jesus, **who promised to send the Advocate**. Holy Mary, Mother of God, pray for us sinners …

3. thy womb, Jesus, **who lifted our human nature into heaven**. Holy Mary, Mother of God, pray for us sinners …

4. thy womb, Jesus, **who spent forty days with the disciples**. Holy Mary, Mother of God, pray for us sinners …

5. thy womb, Jesus, **taken up by a cloud**. Holy Mary, Mother of God, pray for us sinners …

6. thy womb, Jesus, **who made the disciples his witnesses**. Holy Mary, Mother of God, pray for us sinners …

7. thy womb, Jesus, **who blessed the disciples**. Holy Mary, Mother of God, pray for us sinners …

8. thy womb, Jesus, **who gave the Great Commission**. Holy Mary, Mother of God, pray for us sinners…

9. thy womb, Jesus, **seated at the right hand of the Father**. Holy Mary, Mother of God, pray for us sinners …

10. thy womb, Jesus. Holy Mary, Mother of God, **witness to the Ascension,** pray for us sinners …

Alternative Invocation
— thy womb, Jesus, **who must go in order to send the Holy Spirit**. Holy Mary, Mother of God, pray for us sinners …

3. Descent of the Holy Spirit

De Montfort suggestion: Jesus filling thee
with the Holy Spirit

1. thy womb, Jesus, **who sent the Holy Spirit on the fiftieth day**. Holy Mary, Mother of God, pray for us sinners …

2. thy womb, Jesus, **who promised to send the Holy Spirit**. Holy Mary, Mother of God, pray for us sinners …

3. thy womb, Jesus, **who breathed on the apostles**. Holy Mary, Mother of God, pray for us sinners …

4. thy womb, Jesus, **giver of gifts**. Holy Mary, Mother of God, pray for us sinners …

5. thy womb, Jesus, **send us the Spirit to renew the face of the earth**. Holy Mary, Mother of God, pray for us sinners …

6. thy womb, Jesus. Holy Mary, Mother of God, **who joined the apostles in the Upper Room,** pray for us sinners …

7. thy womb, Jesus. Holy Mary, Mother of God, **present at Pentecost,** pray for us sinners …

8. thy womb, Jesus. Holy Mary, Mother of God, **who persevered in prayer with the disciples,** pray for us sinners …

9. thy womb, Jesus. Holy Mary, Mother of God, **on whom the Holy Spirit descended at the Annunciation,** pray for us sinners …

10. thy womb, Jesus. Holy Mary, Mother of God, **spouse of the Holy Spirit,** pray for us sinners …

ALTERNATIVE INVOCATION
— thy womb, Jesus, **who said he had to ascend before the Advocate could come**. Holy Mary, Mother of God, pray for us sinners …

4. Assumption of the Blessed Virgin Mary

De Montfort suggestion: Jesus raising thee up

---

1. thy womb, Jesus, **who assumed his mother into heaven**. Holy Mary, Mother of God, pray for us sinners…

2. thy womb, Jesus. Holy Mary, Mother of God, **highly favored lady,** pray for us sinners …

3. thy womb, Jesus. Holy Mary, Mother of God, **who fell asleep**, pray for us sinners …

4. thy womb, Jesus. Holy Mary, Mother of God, **assumed into heaven,** pray for us sinners …

5. thy womb, Jesus. Holy Mary, Mother of God, **assumed body and soul,** pray for us sinners ...

6. thy womb, Jesus. Holy Mary, Mother of God, **unblemished in all ways,** pray for us sinners ...

7. thy womb, Jesus. Holy Mary, Mother of God, **who did not experience the corruption of the tomb,** pray for us sinners ...

8. thy womb, Jesus. Holy Mary, Mother of God, **the glory of Jerusalem,** pray for us sinners ...

9. thy womb, Jesus. Holy Mary, Mother of God, **splendid boast of our race,** pray for us sinners ...

10. thy womb, Jesus. Holy Mary, Mother of God, **image of the Church**, pray for us sinners ...

5. Coronation of Mary

De Montfort suggestion: Jesus crowning thee

<hr>

1. thy womb Jesus, **King of the Universe**. Holy Mary, Mother of God, pray for us sinners ...

2. thy womb Jesus, **who crowned his mother**. Holy Mary, Mother of God, pray for us sinners ...

3. thy womb Jesus. Holy Mary, Mother of God, **reigning with her son,** pray for us sinners ...

4. thy womb Jesus. Holy Mary, Mother of God, **the Queen Mother,** pray for us sinners ...

5. thy womb Jesus. Holy Mary, Mother of God, **the majestic Queen,** pray for us sinners …

6. thy womb Jesus. Holy Mary, Mother of God, **Queen of Heaven and Earth,** pray for us sinners …

7. thy womb Jesus. Holy Mary, Mother of God, **Queen of Peace,** pray for us sinners …

8. thy womb Jesus. Holy Mary, Mother of God, **Queen of Families,** pray for us sinners …

9. thy womb Jesus. Holy Mary, Mother of God, **Queen of the Holy Rosary,** pray for us sinners …

10. thy womb Jesus. Holy Mary, Mother of God, **Queen of the Clergy,** pray for us sinners …

ALTERNATIVE INVOCATIONS

— thy womb Jesus. Holy Mary, Mother of God, **Queen of Apostles,** pray for us sinners …

— thy womb Jesus. Holy Mary, Mother of God, **Queen of Prophets,** pray for us sinners …

— thy womb Jesus. Holy Mary, Mother of God, **Queen of Saints,** pray for us sinners …

About the Author

Father Edward Lee Looney was ordained a priest for the Diocese of Green Bay June 6, 2015. A member of the Mariological Society of America, he publishes regularly in theological journals, and his writings have appeared in *Catholic Digest* and online at Catholic Exchange and Aleteia. He is well-known for his work popularizing devotion to the National Shrine of Our Lady of Good Help, site of an American-approved 1859 Marian apparition in Champion, Wisconsin. In addition to his devotional writings, he is the author of *A Heart Like Mary's: 31 Daily Meditations to Help You Live and Love as She Does*. To learn more, visit his website: http://www.edwardlooney.com.